THE LITTLE BOOK OF AGA TIPS 3

RICHARD MAGGS

THE LITTLE BOOK OF

AGA TIPS 3

RICHARD MAGGS

A.
Absolute Press

First published in Great Britain in 2004 by
Absolute Press
Scarborough House, 29 James Street West
Bath BA1 2BT, England
Phone 44 (0) 1225 316013 **Fax** 44 (0) 1225 445836
E-mail info@absolutepress.co.uk
Web www.absolutepress.co.uk

A catalogue record of this book is available
from the British Library

ISBN 1 904573 19 3

Printed and bound in Italy by Lego Print

‘Owners, you will find, come to talk
about and regard their Aga as though
it were almost another member of
the household – a fond personality
which has won their affections.
Servants love it. So do I.
And so, I feel sure, would you.
Won’t you come and see it?’

W. T. Wren, M.D. of Aga Heat Ltd

1933 Aga brochure

1

For Aga French toast,

take slightly dry bread, remove the crusts and dip into sugared milk and then beaten egg. Cook on a buttered piece of Bake-O-Glide on the simmering plate, turn over and serve sprinkled with a little caster sugar and cinnamon or maple syrup which has been warmed on the Aga.

2

For quick and easy cheese on toast for one, place grated cheese on a medium slice of bread and place in the centre of the simmering plate on a circle of Bake-O-Glide. Sprinkle over a little paprika, then lower the lid. The underside will toast and the cheese will melt in the heat from the lid.

3

Dry your plain cast iron **pans** or exposed cast iron ground bases in the warmth of the Aga **to prevent rusting.** Use the top plate or warming plate on a four oven cooker. The warming and simmering ovens may also be used.

4

If not needed immediately,

keep takeaways hot

by removing any plastic wrapping and placing the whole paper package to keep hot in the warming or simmering oven for up to two hours until wanted. Don't forget to put plates to warm.

5

Have your Aga maintained regularly.

This is an annual service for gas, and every six months for oil. For electric models, the night storage Aga should have an annual electrical safety check and inspection; a five-year safety check is all that is required for the 13 Amp models.

6

When steaming or boiling a pudding in an aluminium pan, add a slice of lemon to the water to

prevent discoloration

of the pan. The benefits of cooking puddings in the simmering oven, after an initial half-hour on the hotplate, are that the covered pan will not require topping up and the kitchen will not become a sauna.

7

An Aga cast iron trivet

is a good investment as it

protects work surfaces

from hot dishes emerging from the ovens. Your Aga kettle can also live on its own trivet near the cooker ready for rapid boiling.

8

Consider installing an old-fashioned overhead pulley clothes airer, which can be used for

drying washing overnight.

Alternatively, use an A-frame airer or old-fashioned clothes-horse for drying washing in front of the Aga. You will save a lot on tumble-dryer running costs.

9

A creamy risotto may be started off on the simmering plate for five minutes and then left to finish off uncovered in the simmering oven. The rice will not require any attention as it absorbs the stock whilst it slowly **cooks to perfection.**

10

Keep laundered tea towels, etc., in cupboards or drawers next to your Aga for a constant and

handy supply of clean and dry linen.

11

Leftover cooked bacon pieces can be cut up and finally crisped in the simmering oven to make

delicious bacon bites

for garnishing salads.

12

Re-heat cooked drop scones

with a brief spell on both sides on the simmering plate with the lid down. Twenty seconds each side is enough.

13

Tins of golden syrup – which have gone hard – **may be softened** on the back of the top plate. Make sure the lid of the tin is loosened first.

14

If you have **cereals that have lost their original crispness,** dry them out by spreading them out on a tray in the simmering oven for a few hours. This also works with biscuits, crackers and crispbreads.

15

When a cold plain shelf is placed in the roasting oven, the food below it is protected from the strong radiant heat from above for approximately 30 minutes.

The lower down

the shelf is placed on the oven runners,

the greater the shielding effect.

This is especially useful when cooking foods requiring maximum protection such as large, deep sponge cakes.

16

As well as using pre-cut pieces of

Bake-O-Glide

made for the Aga accessories and the Aga Cake Baker, cut up a roll of Bake-O-Glide to

customise your collection of bakeware and make preparing parchment linings a thing of the past.

17

Food containers
made of all sorts of materials
can be safely placed in the simmering and warming ovens
without fear of damage. Plain and foil-lined paper bags and card containers are also safe in these ovens. You can also use anything which is dishwasher-proof such as boilable plastic and Pyrex jugs and mixing bowls.

18

A ceramic spoon rest is useful to

save making a mess on the top plate

when repeatedly stirring and testing foods cooking on the top of the cooker. Acidic foods such as milk and fruit juice can damage vitreous enamel, so this is especially useful in the jam and preserving season.

19

Once you have started to **sauté onions and garlic,** transfer the covered pan to the simmering oven for 20 minutes to finish softening **without any attention.** Return the pan to the hotplate to drive off the excess liquid which will have collected. Then brown the onions, if necessary, before continuing with your recipe.

20

If you find rich fruit cakes take too long to cook

using the slow method in your simmering oven, add only a quarter of the alcohol specified in the recipe and use the remainder to 'feed' the underside of the finished cake.

21

When you **slow cook rich fruit cakes** in a cool Aga simmering oven, always start checking for doneness ahead of time – an inserted skewer should come out clean when the cake is cooked.

A quick guide is to allow one hour per inch (2.5cm) for a round cake and one and a quarter-hours per inch for square cakes. Bake on an Aga toaster on the floor of the oven.

22

Kippers are best cooked

on a grill rack in the high position in a roasting tin placed on the highest set of runners in the roasting oven. As with all oven-cooked fish, the strong odours are ducted safely away through the oven vent.

23

Toast Mexican tortillas

Toast Mexican tortillas dry on a lightly greased simmering plate. Fry cooked tortilla wedges in a little oil in a roasting tin on the floor of the roasting oven to serve with drinks. Tired leftover tortilla chips which have become softened can be refreshed with a short spell in the simmering oven.

24

Oven-roasted vegetables are fantastic in the Aga. Cut them all up in similar sizes and place in an Aga roasting tin, drizzle with olive oil and seasoning and toss well **with garlic and herbs** such as rosemary. Leave to marinate if possible. Roast on the floor of the roasting oven, shaking the contents every so often until they are just tender.

25

Try freezing

risen **bread dough**

in bread tins or as rolls as soon as proving has taken place. When frozen, store in plastic bags in the freezer until required. When wanted, remove from the freezer and allow to defrost,

then bake freshly.

26

Home-made

granola-style breakfast cereals

can easily be made by drying out the well-tossed mix of oats, nuts, raisins, maple syrup, etc., on trays in the simmering and warming ovens.

27

If you have **canine or feline Aga worshippers,**

on oil and gas fired models, periodically check inside the outer burner door for accumulated hair and fluff. Gently remove with a soft brush between servicing, but don't be tempted to use a vacuum cleaner on a working cooker.

28

Once you have thoroughly

cleaned paintbrushes,

suspend them in a jam jar with elastic bands and leave at the back of the top plate to dry thoroughly with

no misshapen bristles.

29

Cook-chill

convenience food

Cooking Guide:

These may be cooked on the grid shelf on the floor of the roasting oven with a cold plain shelf above. Prick or remove the film as directed and allow 75% of the time recommended for conventional ovens before checking it is thoroughly cooked. Serve or keep hot in the simmering or warming ovens until wanted.

30

Walnuts shell easily if they are warmed in the simmering oven for 20 minutes before cracking. Use a ratchet nutcracker to ensure whole kernels are extracted and rub off the skins in a clean tea towel.

31

Seal the freshly cut ends of

nylon cord

and rope for gardening and boating needs. Twist the fibres to a point and dab on the boiling plate to fuse the ends

to prevent fraying.

32

When making casseroles

and ragoûts that have a high fat content, such as a rich oxtail stew or *Osso Bucco*, refrigerate the cooked dish to

enable the removal of the solidified fat

before re-heating and serving the next day. The flavour is also often improved with this method.

33

To prolong the life of your kettle,

don't leave it full of water when not being used, especially overnight. Always use freshly drawn water when making tea and only fill as much as you need for the fastest boiling

34

Break up **dry stale bread scraps** into marble-sized pieces and leave for several hours in the simmering or warming ovens to dry **for dog meal.**

35

Keep a wooden saltbox or pottery 'salt pig' near your Aga **for free-flowing dry salt** to season your cooking. I prefer Malden or the French *fleur de sel*. *Guérande* or *Halen Môn* are also worth seeking out.

36

If your simmering plate is a little hot, raise the insulating lid for ten minutes to allow it to cool slightly while making your recipe. It will then be at the perfect temperature for cooking delicious

drop scones, Welshcakes, pikelets and crumpets.

37

Pastry cases do not need to be baked blind in an Aga. Place the flan dish directly onto the floor of the roasting oven, and pour in the filling immediately. Metal, Pyrex and porcelain dishes may all be used and you will achieve

crisp pastry cases with perfectly set fillings.

38

A quick way to dry-fry spices

before grinding is to pre-heat a cast iron pan on the floor of the roasting oven for five minutes – an Aga frying pan is ideal. Transfer to the simmering plate, add the spices and shake the pan every ten seconds until lightly toasted.

39

Melt butter in a dish at the back of the top plate ready to dress freshly cooked vegetables for

an attractive finish before sending to table.

Wash and prepare parsley ahead of time but chop finely at the last minute for the best colour.

40

Demijohns of

wine will ferment well

in the nurturing warmth of the Aga. Leave on a work surface next to the cooker, or if you are a keen winemaker, designate an area next to the cooker for this purpose.

41

Clarify butter and

make your own ghee. Place a pack of unsalted butter in a basin in the simmering oven for 30 minutes. Remove and allow to cool a little. Skim off the white foam, and pour off the clear ghee, discarding the milk solids left behind.

42

To roast and skin hazelnuts,

place the shelled nuts in a cast iron pan on the floor of the roasting oven for 3-4 minutes, shaking the pan every so often. When pale golden, cool and place in a clean tea towel. Fold around the nuts and rub firmly to remove the papery skins.

43

Children's paintings,

collages and appliqué masterpieces

will quickly dry

out on a tray on an Aga Chef's pad on top of the simmering plate lid. *Papier-mâché* models require a slower period of drying on a worktop near the Aga.

44

Boil pasta

in plenty of well-salted water in a large open pan on the boiling plate

until *al dente*.

I recommend the Aga stainless steel stock pot, which is ideal. Alternatively, boil for three minutes on top, then transfer, covered, to the simmering oven for a further seven minutes.

45

When having a baking session with a two oven Aga,

succession bake using a falling oven:

start with baking bread and pastry requiring a hot oven, then cook biscuits needing a more moderate temperature, finishing with any cakes which require a very moderate oven.

46

For a simple yet

highly efficient laundry aid,

fit a rail on the wall or ceiling above your Aga for hanging ironed shirts to air, and to allow wet jackets to dry.

47

A few inexpensive cork mats are invaluable to use to **protect the top plate** when warming teapots and gravy boats without scratching the enamel. Aga chef's pads are invaluable for protecting metal or enamel insulating lids.

48

Always rinse out a milk pan

with cold water before using it to heat up milk on the simmering plate. After use, soak immediately in cold water. Both these tips make washing-up much easier.

49

Sterilise sieved topsoil

for home-made seedling compost by baking in the roasting oven for 30 minutes. Use an old roasting tin reserved for the purpose, or a plain unpainted biscuit tin.

50

Dry your own flowers

for attractive out-of-season arrangements and to make your own *pot-pourri*. Hang bunches over the Aga rail or place, securely hooked, onto the wall above your cooker.

Acknowledgments

My thanks to all my family, friends, colleagues, fellow chefs and, of course, Aga owners everywhere for their constant support and encouragement. To everyone at Aga-Rayburn; it is a pleasure to continue to work with such an enthusiastic group of people. Also, a huge thank you to my publisher, Jon Croft, and my editor and graphic designer, Matt Inwood, at Absolute Press who are now great friends and fellow Aga louts.

AGA is a registered trademark of Aga Foodservice Group plc.

Bake-O-Glide™ is a re-usable non-stick coated cooking material, available from Aga Specialists.

Richard Maggs

A dynamic and accomplished chef,
Richard is an authority on Aga cookery.
As well as having featured on TV and radio,
he writes for several magazines and contributes
a regular column to the official Aga Magazine.
A bestselling author, he is also the resident
Aga cookery expert, The Cookery Doctor,
with the award-winning Agalinks website at
www.agalinks.com.

A selected list of Aga titles from Absolute Press

Also by Richard Maggs
The Complete Book of Aga Know-How (8.99)
The essential get-to-know-your-Aga book.

Tim James
Aga: The Story of a Kitchen Classic (£30)
The beautifully illustrated, definitive 80-year history of a kitchen icon.

Louise Walker's *Traditional Aga* titles
The bestselling Traditional Aga *series: essential for every Aga cook.*

The Traditional Aga Cookery Book (£9.95)
The Traditional Aga Party Book (£9.95)
The Traditional Aga Book of Slow Cooking (£9.95)
The Traditional Aga Box Set (*all three titles above*) (£29.50)
The Traditional Aga Four Seasons Cookery Book (£9.95)
The Traditional Aga Book of Vegetarian Cooking (£9.95)

Laura James' New Aga Cook books
A contemporary collection of recipes for today's Aga cook.

The New Aga Cook: Fast (7.99)
The New Aga Cook: Kids (7.99)
The New Aga Cook: Weekends (7.99)

THE LITTLE BOOK OF AGA TIPS

'Full of winning ideas for Aga owners.'
The Times

'Aga Tips is splendid! The best tip is about warming immovable jam jar lids – brilliant!'
Marjorie Dunkels, Aga owner